W9-ADD-474

What a Modern Catholic Believes About WORSHIP

by C. J. McNaspy

THE THOMAS MORE ASSOCIATION
180 N. Wabash Ave.
Chicago, Ill. 60601

Standard Book Number: 0–88347–031–4

For Maurice Lavanoux
Pioneer in all things liturgical

CONTENTS

INTRODUCTION

When the invitation came to contribute to this series, my first impulse was to accept; it was flattering, especially in view of the big names of previous contributors. A quick second thought brought me back to reality: How could I presume to give *the* modern Catholic's viewpoint on liturgy, or anything else, for that matter? What made me reconsider was a more careful reading of the title. It said *a* modern Catholic, not *the* modern Catholic. That made the decisive difference, since anyone who reads and reflects can fancy himself a modern Catholic, even if he is a generation older than his fellow contributors. I hope they will not be too chagrined.

Why yet another book on liturgy? Isn't there a surfeit already, to which I have made perhaps too many additions? My resolution of this scruple took two forms. One, as benefits my age, may be labeled authoritarian: After all, the editors should know whether such a need exists, since this is part of their job. The other: Popular thinking on the liturgy is in such turmoil that just possibly a simple, pedestrian, unpolemical attempt to find bits of consensus and order may prove useful. Liturgiologists and professional *avant garde* theologians will, if they bother to pick up this tiny volume, discover nothing recondite or new, save in the appendix, most of which I did not write.[1]

I have been fortunate to live in a university where the liturgy is very much alive, and where discussion on the subject is more creative than polarized. This may account for what may be found to be a tonality of optimism. Liturgical styles here range over a healthy spectrum from the very traditional to the thoroughly progressive, with no hurling of epithets or counterepithets. A strong charismatic (pentecostal) movement enlivens the campus, guided by such nationally respected leaders as Patti Gallagher, Donald Gelpi and Harold Cohen. At the same time, regular "supply" ensures corrective contact with the nonacademic world and with Christians of less sophistication or none whatever. Thus, I hope that my reflections will not be dubbed ivory-tower and instantly dismissed.

My practical interest in liturgy started some 35 years ago, when I first came to know Father Gerald Ellard. Like many of us back in the thirties, I may be said to have "backed into" the subject, starting with music, which remains my major interest. The problem of the vernacular early engaged my attention, and two dissertations dealt with the problem.[2]

It would be impossible, even if it were worthwhile, to mention all the people to whom I am grateful for shaping my liturgical ideas. The list would start with Josef Jungmann, Godfrey Diekmann, William Leonard, and would surely include such younger theologians as Donald J. Martin (now at Notre Dame) and Joseph Laishley (teaching at Heythrop, London). Long conversations with these two proved the immediate stimulus to the present book.

One hopes that "a modern Catholic" will not be judged

less modern for having recourse to an ancient formula in organizing the ideas here presented: "What, why, when, where, who, how." It so happened that only after they were jotted down did I avert to an old mnemonic Latin hexameter: "Quis, quid, ubi, quibus auxiliis, cur, quomodo, quando." As this popped out of my unconscious I was reminded, as the reader doubtless will frequently be, that one doesn't easily shake off one's past.

Chapter One

WHAT

WHAT, then, is liturgy? A sign of contradiction today, the cynic might suggest. For the very term, a rare one as recently as a decade ago, is now likely to raise hackles, even sow division rather than stand as a sign of union and communion.

The text books offer a handy definition: "public worship." So far we are on sturdy, uncontroversial ground. Vatican Council II took up the matter in its first session, and in its very first document described liturgy as "the outstanding means by which the faithful can express in their lives, and manifest to others, the mystery of Christ and the real nature of the true Church" (*Constitution on the Sacred Liturgy* #2).[1]

Since Dec. 4, 1963, when the *Constitution* was promulgated (I was fortunate enough to be in St. Peter's basilica at the time), volumes and volumes have poured out expanding on this description.[2]

Despite this, or possibly because of this, a widespread malaise regarding liturgy has overtaken Catholics at large. It is hard to realize that just a few years ago most Catholics simply went to Mass, mainly on Sundays, and in their several ways fulfilled what they had learned to be a serious obligation. Today, if not bored with the subject, they are likely to entertain strong, even bitter feelings, whenever they think of liturgy or hear it discussed. The polarization that ensues makes it difficult to remember what liturgy is really all about.

Some clearing of the air surrounding the word would thus seem to be in order. Let us first examine what at least one "modern Catholic" believes liturgy is *not.*

It is not, I believe, a group-dynamic or "T" session. Reacting against the baroque formalistic concept of liturgy, many eager chaplains and other priests sometimes sound or act as though it were mainly a sort of beautiful get-together, a group encounter, a therapeutic to alienation and isolation. This is not to suggest that none or even all of these are not elements in liturgy, causes or by-products. For liturgy, in order to be fully effective, must not be or seem cold, abstract, impersonal, merely objective. It must be (however suspicious one may be of the jargonish sound of the words) warm, authentic, personal, interpersonal and, yes, relevant.

Even less, perhaps, is liturgy some sort of show, spectacle, sacred concert or extravaganza. The old-style pontifical High Mass did afford a certain awe, grandeur, sense of mystery and the sacral. In an often drab world, it offered elements of color, uplift, glory. In today's world of incessant stimulation and TV titillation, the young, at least, may be inclined to yawn and be totally "turned off." They have seen more spectacular television commercials.

Nor is liturgy a mere set of ceremonies with highly personal resonances, an instrument of instant spiritual consolation. While there is certainly room and need for this, suggested by the contemporary enthusiasm for yoga and other oriental techniques of spirituality, liturgy is a corrective, countervalent communitarian action. We do approach God as individuals, but Holy Scripture has more to say about our responsibilities as the People of God. Even in personal prayer, we are "our brother's keepers." The charismatic movement, despite occasional eccentricities, involves the Christian in far more than spiritual self-indulgence or solipsistic satisfaction. So should a vital liturgy.

It would be myopic in the extreme to think of liturgy as merely a juridical obligation, or even some sort of innate religious necessity. Religiosity has taken many forms, some of them far from edifying. There is even some sense in the notion that Christianity is opposed to "religion." Yet, Christ came neither to destroy the Law nor to destroy all religious impulses; it may be said that he turned the whole thing inside out. In him religion becomes both God-centered and man-centered, but not self-centered, much less a subtler form of egoism.

This suggests that liturgy, in the Christian sense, cannot be simply a creative reading session. Granted some place for Teilhardian or other contemporary spiritual readings, perhaps in the course of homilies or shared reflections; the focus must always be on Holy Scripture, the privileged reading *par excellence.* In liturgy we uncover, not our idiosyncratic preferences, but the Word of God, with its high promises and stern demands.

No more can liturgy be thought of purely as spontaneous prayer. Anyone who has been present at certain types of small-group liturgies knows the peril of highly articulate priests, eloquently and lengthily expanding in self-expression. I recall one such occasion, when the articulate young priest improvised passionately for over an hour, leaving only five minutes or so for the eucharistic prayer. The rest of us felt helpless, intimidated by this new form of clericalism, indulged in by a man who honestly thought himself to be anticlerical (in the old but hardly worse sense).

More positively, without pretending to cover grounds that may be found more adequately covered in larger and deeper books, one may suggest briefly that liturgy is our worship as incarnate, corporate, social beings. It does correspond to a God-given set of creaturely needs. It expresses our relationship to God and to one another. Solidarity is as human a thing as is the experience of identity. If the pun be forgiven, even the Mass bell tolls for thee.

It has often been pointed out that Christianity (much like Judaism, but with the important peak of the Incarnation) is an historical religion. It incorporates us into the Christ of the Mystical Body, but not as though the historical Jesus were irrelevant or merely historical. Revelation is not merely something of the now, but has occurred at specific times over some millennia. Nor did it all happen at once; rather, it is worked out in human and sacred history.

Thus our worship, like our faith, cannot escape from tradition (literally, what has been handed on). True, much of what used to pass as tradition was mere routine, with no organic links to Revelation itself. Still, there remain certain elements of Christian worship without which the act becomes, if not nugatory, at least maimed. For all the possible diversity in liturgy, for there to be a true Eucharist there must be some reflection and re-enactment of the Last Supper and its setting. The Last Supper, even though it was not celebrated in Latin with Jesus facing away from the disciples, was still no casual picnic. Nor can the Eucharist be thought of as simply a companionable partaking of food and drink, a Christianized cocktail party. It must be the expression in terms of Eucharistic prayer of what the Eucharist means.

This, in brief, implies an experience of praise and thanksgiving to the Father, through his Son, as we remember and re-enact sacramentally the fundamental events of Revelation: God's creative and redemptive work. Such an experience obviously is more than an individualistic enterprise; it is one shared in and expressive of the whole church. While we remain individuals, we somehow become more than mere individuals in our response to God's initiative. Our posture, then, must be sensitive to our role in the priestly people of God.

This further suggests that it is not fully Christian to think of community as a column on the march, looking neither to the right or left. The elongated church, especially with that rather recent innovation the pew, promotes such a feeling, as though we looked toward God with little awareness of each other. The advantages of such a structure are obvious, akin to those of a movie house; but the disadvantages are not less real, and probably overriding. The pre-basilican church was more central, as indeed was the church we find especially in the East.

Regardless of architecture, however, our liturgical concept should draw more on Christ's words: "Whenever two or three are gathered in my name, there I am in the midst of them." In liturgy we think of God not as "out there," but as within us, present to us as community.

Further, it is not theologically sound to think of liturgy

as something totally self-contained, merely the community at prayer. Liturgy, to be living, must flow over into life. It must be the source and focus of activity.[3] The very term Mass means etymologically a sending, a commission. The Christian life, to be sure, begins and ends in prayer, but the prayer must accompany and impregnate action. Christ's challenges are unambiguous: "Not everyone who says 'Lord, Lord' . . . Love thy neighbor as thyself," and the like. Liturgical prayer can never rest in self-contentment or even the most devout-sounding quietism.[4]

Chapter Two

WHY

In a sense, the question, "Why liturgy?" has already been answered. We are, as noted above, "incarnate, corporate, social beings." In a word, we are (as Pascal acutely observed) neither angel nor beast. We know little about angels, except that according to theory they are quite spiritual and according to Thomas Aquinas unique each in his/her own species. A lonely breed at best.

But most animals are gregarious, and our language is rich in terms for such groups (flock, pride, school, shoal, team, trip, yoke, pack, drove, cry, brace, gam, grist, hive, leap, knot, litter, muster, nye or pod; depending on whether one is a sheep, a lion, fish, pilchard, duck, ox, wolf, sheep, hound, duck, whale, bee, leopard, toad, pig, peacock, pheasant or seal). Whatever our groupings, as men/women we are, in this respect, somewhat closer to our animal brethren. The hermit—religious or otherwise—remains the odd man out. Man, in the old description, is quite fundamentally a social animal.

This is not to depreciate the values attendant upon solitude, when solitude is embraced as a temporary state in favor of deepened reflection. Spiritual retreats, provided they are directed (and thus not entirely solitary), remain and will remain an inescapable step in spiritual growth. Nobody, so far as I know, holds that all prayer or meditation must always be a group activity. If, in the past, solitude may have been overestimated, surely in the more recent past it has been falsely denigrated.[1]

Still, the normal human condition has a strong social dimension. We need each other, not least at crucial moments of our lives. I personally can never forget how intensely I felt this reality some winters ago when I became lost, after midnight, in the Alps during a blizzard. It is the experience, we have reason to believe, of everyone when facing the moment of death; hence, the human and sacramental urgency for the Sacrament of the Sick—a social sacrament, not less than the others.

But as soon as two or three are gathered (whether in Jesus' name or not), the freedom or irresponsibility of total solitude must yield to the freedom and need of others. What G. B. Shaw said about the freedom or nonfreedom of smokers or nonsmokers in the same railroad coach has pertinence here. So long as I pray alone, my spontaneity or sense of the impromptu need know few bounds. Whether I prostrate or kneel or dance or gesticulate matters little, except as an expression of my prayerful feelings.

However, when others are present some of the liberty otherwise enjoyed must be restrained, out of respect for my fellow humans. This leads ineluctably to rules, either explicit or with the implicitness of good manners. Respect for others thus becomes a basic law of liturgy. Indeed, it might be said that all liturgical rules (or rubrics) are oriented toward the rights of others, the community. Private prayer, having few direct social implications, needs little or no regulation.

It is hard to remember that just a decade ago the liturgy was meticulously regulated, even as regards the number of inches the priest might hold his hands apart, or the different decibels he might use when saying the collect, the Sanctus, or the Canon (three quite different sound levels). The severity with which these rules were interpreted was obviously excessive; yet the element of control or balance or restraint made sense. Although certain rubrics had outworn their usefulness or meaning, the idea behind them was sound; reverence really toward others—enabling them to worship without undue annoyance or encumbrance caused by others.

Today we are less inclined to worry about rubrics, as though minutiae had little place in worship. The new attitude is doubtless a healthier one, more suggestive of the liberty of the children of God than of pharasaical tightness. Today's mind-set is more in the direction of casualness, perhaps even a cult of casualness. In daily life our manners are less formal when they are not downright crude. Nor, I suppose, would many wish to return to top hats, uncomfortable clothes, elaborate etiquette in general. The gain in casualness has often reflected a growth in candor and honesty.

However, even Woodstock (which now seems so long ago) had its own rules or rubrics. The most casual groupings insist on certain rules of the games. Primitive tribes, far from being totally free, are known to be most exigent in tribal custom and almost ruthless in punishment for infractions. This, I believe, arises out of a conscious or preconscious awareness that structure is needed if society is not to self-destruct. Ritual, anthropologists tell us, is part of every society.

To be sure, present-day social rituals have changed a great deal since our grandparents' time. Our courtesies are less elaborate, our garb (however manipulated by Madison Avenue we may still be) less formal. We find it hard to put up with lengthy, repetitious graduation exercises. Yet, who would want to do away altogether with some symbol of graduation? Not being angels, we still need some sense of ceremony, some visible-aural symbol that something important is happening.

This is all the more so when we come to our encounters with God as the People of God. At such a transcendent moment as marriage, bride and groom may not want the Wagner or Mendelssohn marches, or rice, or a multiplicity of attendants; but they want something symbolic of the sacred event. We have seen or heard of bizarre ceremonies (like marriage on an iceberg, to suggest the greater depths unseen), but ceremony of some sort is instinctively demanded. It is not a regression toward magic to recognize this deep human need.[2]

It is quite possible that we have come to a dead end in demythologization, or desacralization, or demystification. Recent students of religion point to the need for myth (not in the sense of falsehood, of course). It is curious that not many years elapsed between Harvey Cox' two volumes *Secular City* and *Feast of Fools,* indicating that rationalization and technocracy could take us just so far. It may be that further plumbing of the universe's manifold complexity has veered us once again toward the sense of mystery—not a return to Comte's prescientific attitudes, but a turn to something deeper than quantification and positivistic explanation.

This may have something to do with the current fad of

occultism and even diabolism. Today's young people, suggests Dean J. Stillson Judah of the Graduate Theological Union in Berkeley, "cannot live without the depth of myth and symbol and the richness of mysticism that existed before the rise of the empirical scientific attitude." If they find this missing in official liturgical situations, they will improvise or take flight into a world of spiritism or a religion of irreligion, perhaps worshiping or fancying they worship Satan himself. How much of the recent cult of the devil is due to latent demonic traits and how much to a playfulness about what is really not believed in, is difficult to judge. But something of the need for cult and the need for mystery can hardly be totally absent.

It is not hard to believe, too, that the phenomenal growth of interest in spectator sports is related to what we are discussing. The ceremonial majesty surrounding professional athletic events—flag, national anthem, intricate marches and the entire ritual of the game itself—is no idle or frivolous panoply. People seem to need great events, even if only athletic events, to be symbolically exalted above the commonplace.

Much the same, too, may be said of "The Cult of Culture," which I described at length in *America* magazine (5/9/64). Today, in greater numbers than ever, young people throng to museums, concerts, films, dramas, in a spirit of celebration and with an absorption akin to religious feeling. In part this may be a surrogate for religion; but in part it is an expression of the need for the transcendent, for exploration into ultimacy or at least a reality not susceptible to mere rationalization.

All of this may sound merely psychological, yet another instance of rationalization. I believe its meaning to be somewhat deeper. We believe, in the terms of our Creed, in *one* God; historically the accent is on *one,* as opposed to a God of good and one of evil. The God who created us and endowed us with human needs and capacities is not other than the God of revelation. Grace, theologians assure us, builds upon nature, since the same God is author of both. Little wonder, then, if our liturgy should correspond to our human demands—demands for ceremony, the sense of solidarity, the respect for our fellows, the awareness and recognition of mystery.

Whatever heaven may be like (and scriptural descriptions use very human images like that of the banquet), our worship of God here on earth needs to be earthy, incarnate, thoroughly embodied, enfleshed. "He who would play the angel," to complete the quotation from Pascal, "will play the beast."[3]

Chapter Three

WHEN

PART of our human situation (again, so far as we know, quite different from that of angels) is our time-conditioning. We live rhythmically, not only in heartbeat, pulse, the systole and distole of breathing, but also in the sequence of day and night, the cycle of seasons even in an air-conditioned world. The break in our circadian rhythms during a Transatlantic flight proves the point.

Unsurprisingly, our patterns of worship also have something to do with time. The human mood of morning is quite distinct from that of evening or midday or night. In line with this reality, worship (not only Christian worship) has always been attuned to temporal rhythms. Even the austerest monks do not pray in the same way at various times of day or year. The Divine Office, chanted in choir, recognizes differences of day and night, Lent and Paschaltide, and the like. In fact, the differentiations observed in monastic choir are so elaborate as to be bewildering to the uninitiated: Matins, Lauds, Prime, Vespers, Compline, etc.

Vatican Council II was insistent on reform of the liturgical calendar. In the course of time, so many feast days had inflated the church year that one could hardly distinguish one day from another. True, there were subtle distinctions between what were called "Doubles"—first class, second class, semi-doubles, and the like. This indicated that not all days were on a par. Yet, there remained a feeling of clutter, with the obscuring of the great days recalling moments of special redemption. A related problem quickly arose.[1]

The problem had doubtless been there for some time, vague and diffused and not yet articulated. It seems related to the very progress of our secular society, our control of nature and of the day-night processes. The week is not quite what it was in a rural society, nor are the seasons. Many people live more by night than by day. Holidays and vacations are more common, and our very emancipation from the consequences of time make it harder and harder to distinguish one day from another, even one season from another. And now we have permission to celebrate Sunday on Saturday.

The long weekend further complicates our rhythm of life. We speak increasingly of "making" or "taking" time, of having a "free" Sunday. With Mass available at almost any hour, we naturally tend to fit it in somehow, in some left-over slot during the weekend. Less and less does it seem the center of Sunday. In many cases it is still looked on as some sort of dull residual obligation, if an obligation at all.

True, Christmas is still very much with us, in part because of the enormous commercial possibilities offered. Schools close for a week or a month, and something similar occurs at Easter, though with far less excitement, despite the church's insistence that the central mystery of our faith and liturgy is Easter. Catholic schools continue to give holidays on certain church feasts, but with no specific celebration geared to the feasts' meaning. Ascension Thursday thus becomes no more than a misplaced Sunday.[2]

There is, I believe, no ready answer or set of answers to the questions implied here. In the broadest sense, what we can do is recognize the value of variety and rhythm in life and worship. In Saint-Exupéry's classic, *The Little Prince,* there occurs a hint that may be of use, and I hope that readers will not mind my quoting it once again. The wise old Fox had just used the word "rite." Whereupon the Little Prince asked what the word meant. The Fox replied: "Rites are things that make one day different from another." Perhaps not a comprehensive definition, but suggestive enough.

Days are already sufficiently if not excessively alike. We need feasts for a number of reasons. Among them is the psychic need for variety. If every day is celebrated at a top degree of intensity it becomes no different from its neighbors. Even millionaires, I imagine, do not live invariably on caviare or pompano-en-papillote; if they did, these delicacies would diminish into commonplaces. Nor can we worship with the same degree of celebration every day.

This is not to say that there can be no such thing, in life or worship, as daily bread. Every culture has its staples, be they concocted of wheat, rice or corn. But every culture also has its days of celebration, of feasting, of special elation. Traditionally, the Western Church's liturgical daily prayers have not been elaborately rhetorical. The Lord's Prayer and the daily Psalms of the Divine Office tend to be rather simple and low-key, while the exuberant Exsultet is reserved to the Easter Vigil.

There is surely place and even need for daily prayer,

and in the spiritual nourishment of many there is, I believe, place for daily Mass. Yet, even at Solesmes Abbey in France, where the traditional Mass is celebrated with a maximum of beautiful music, distinctions are made. On simpler days simpler chants are used. Not even the most ardent devotee of Gregorian chant could respond daily to the same masterpieces, any more than serious musicians could meaningfully hear Bach's B Minor Mass every day, or every week, for that matter. (Hence the appalling barbarity of the newscast that appropriated the Scherzo of Beethoven's Ninth Symphony as its daily signature; accordingly, I for one have long since switched to another network.)

Hence, too, the need for a greater variety of Eucharistic prayers. As long as the Roman Mass was said in Latin, we could afford to use the same prayer every day, since most people couldn't understand it anyway, and priests, if devout, found ways to make it somehow devotional. But today, with the vernacular, we cannot fully respond to the same Eucharistic prayer every day, or even to the same four prayers if we go to Mass frequently.

By the time this is published we may have many more official Eucharistic prayers, fitting different needs and moods of the liturgical calendar. Meantime, a wide number of such prayers have been created, with different degrees of success, to help fit the need. In a number of liturgical centers and on various campuses we find serious attempts to solve the problem of monotony and routine.[3]

Yet even within the strictest interpretation of present liturgical directives there is considerable leeway. A priest endowed with taste and imagination may take advantage of options currently offered. There is no need whatever for Mass to be said exactly the same way every day. Even an uncreative person, if graced with Christian humility, can today supply healthy variety, provided he plans carefully and consults the laity or other priests. Every parish, at least in cities, includes persons of taste and experience in communication. Too often, however, these gifted people are given no opportunity to share their gifts with others and return them to God in public worship.

Sacred time can be rescued, too, in other ways. Lawrence E. Moser's volume, *Home Celebrations,* offers more than thirty home rituals that require no special permission. Prayers and ceremonies modeled roughly on those of the official liturgy can celebrate and sanctify such family moments as birth, moving to a new home, engagements, departures, retirements, the visit of relatives, graduations, birthdays, anniversaries—events that punctuate life and give it special meaning. One hopes that this book will be widely used and will prod other creative persons into providing us with more such hints for celebration.[4]

Another aspect of time calls for brief discussion—that of leisure, called by Joseph Pieper and others *The Basis of Culture,* sacred and secular. Happily, in recent years Sunday Masses are being rescheduled beyond the rigid 60-minute hour, and no longer do people have to find parking space and rush in and out of church to allow others to find parking space. But there is still need for leisure before, during and after important ceremonies. The encounter with God is not something to be treated like a television hour or half-hour show.

A more appropriate analogy would seem to me (perhaps because of my orientation toward music) the symphony concert. To enjoy such a concert fully we arrive well before the beginning, we relax and settle into our places, we reflect on what is about to happen by glancing at the program notes, we wait in creative expectation. As the orchestra members move toward their seats, expectation rises. The concertmaster appears, receives tentative applause, signals the oboist to provide the note A, to which all others tune. Then a great hush before the conductor appears, accepts applause, raises his baton for total attention. Only then does the ceremony begin.

The rituals surrounding athletic contests—whether Superbowl or high school competition—are hardly less solemn. Some of this as suggested above may be seen as part of our need for ritual, but some of it is doubtless the sense of time and preparation. We need this for full awareness.[5]

In a word, we need to give some thought to resisting the forces and pressures that shape us. A sort of spiritual ecology is imperative, to cleanse the environment of an endless rush and artificially induced excitement. Our lives cannot be an incessant round of peak experiences, or the experiences will no longer be peak. Reflection, leisure, a respect for the normal rhythm of life must in some way be recaptured. This is not to turn the clock back, but to allow it to move ahead at a truly human pace.

Chapter Four

WHERE

IF WE are conditioned by time, we are no less, or only slightly less, conditioned by space. As a person who has frequently flown for the past forty years and has logged well over a million miles on all continents, I am quite aware that place does not occupy the same importance that it did, say, when my parents were my age. It was not long ago, for example, that I finished an afternoon class in New Orleans, flew to Washington for the Bernstein *Mass* premiere, then back for the next morning's classes in New Orleans. If this occurs in the life of a mere teacher, how familiar the pattern is to the cosmopolitan businessman who commutes between New York and London.

For all this, however, I have met no one who travels extensively and fails to complain of the jet lag, and the discomfort of sleeping in a different hotel room on successive nights. For all our contemporary nomadism, we still have some sense of place. The "global village" may be all very well when it comes to newscasts, but all of us retain some sense of home, which is to say of place.

Modern apartments, too, tend toward the multipurpose —living rooms quickly convertible into places for eating, and the like. Yet, paradoxically, we recognize the transitory benefits of specialized places; we use funeral parlors and restaurants and country clubs, rather than attempt to do everything at home. For important events, at least, we sense the value of spatial differentiation.

Place becomes increasingly imporant in what may be called a nostalgic way. It was not too long ago that I first visited certain ancestral lands—Ireland, for example, France and Italy. If not a minor Antaeus returning to native earth to regain strength, one at least felt some sense of rootedness by walking where one's ancestors had walked. In a little volume on Europe published some years ago, I entitled an early chapter "Going Home to Europe."[1] For little as one may prefer to remain in an ancestral home, hardly anyone is not a bit eager to visit there, in some way with a sense of pilgrimage.

So it is that we feel a sense of place in the matter of religion. It is not only Jews who make the pilgrimage to the Holy Land. Vicariously I could join the thrill of my Jewish compatriots last summer when first visiting the citadel of Masada, where the Zealots had held out so heroically against the conquering Romans. Everyone who visits Jerusalem, be he Christian or Jew, feels the impulse to kiss ground that has been uniquely blessed. Nor is the experience of reading the Sermon on the Mount near the Sea of Galilee mainly one of nature appreciation. The place itself, one realizes, is more than simply lovely.

Granted that attachment to holy places can be excessive or take extravagant forms. In the Holy Land, for example, one meets guides who are only too eager to answer all questions about exact spots—to tell you exactly where Jesus fell under the cross for the first or third time. As Eliade has suggested, there seems to be some inner need to find the exact holy place where some divine intervention or communication, some hierophany has taken place. Pilgrims, over the years, have cherished these spots (real or supposed). No one, of course, knows exactly where the Ascension took place; nonetheless, a Crusader church (now under Moslem control) marks the spot, and the custodian will show you—as his predecessors did to St. Francis and St. Ignatius—the very footmarks of Jesus as he ascended. One may be tempted to smile at such specificity; but the instinct is deeply human and deserves respect.

Pilgrimage, whether sacred or secular, is thus a part of our social inheritance. The millions of tourists who throng to Washington, or Gettysburg, or Lexington, have some awareness of this. But those who save money for years to visit Bethlehem, Nazareth and Jerusalem are following an inner summons that goes back to St. Helena, the early pilgrim Etheria, the thousands who risked life or freedom to walk where Christ walked. And Moslems reckon pilgrimage to Mecca as one of the five "pillars" of Islam; even daily, every time they pray they turn toward Mecca, as a sacred place where God came into contact with man.

Christianity, rooted as deeply in place as in time, has never overlooked this human reality. Granted that the time would come when men would worship God neither on Mount Gerizim nor in the temple of Jerusalem, but "in spirit and truth," and that what really matters is the interior rather than the superficial. Still, the early church venerated the spots where Peter and Paul were martyred. Even today, when visiting the catacombs—especially that of St. Priscilla, where the earliest Christian art goes back to the second century—one feels something of the awesome, the numinous, hardly experienced elsewhere. My most sophisticated friends have acknowledged this, too.

If I have stressed this rather elementary fact, it is mainly because of a current feeling that it doesn't matter where the Eucharist is celebrated. In many ways it doesn't. Some liturgical celebrations that I have found most personally moving have taken place in unlikely surroundings—like a spartan hotel room in Russia. And by now most American Catholics must have known the warmth of small-group liturgies in a home situation, with little or none of the panoply usually surrounding church celebrations. After one or other of these experiences, who has not said or thought: Church was never like this, was it?

Nor would I, for one, ever want to return to the rigidity of nothing but church liturgies. The advantages of intimacy and community felt in harmonious, friendly, small groups are too real to be discounted. I believe that this style of liturgy will grow rather than diminish in frequency within the foreseeable future. One cannot always withdraw into the ease of noncommittal anonymity associated with large-group ceremonies. The very effort expended when the group is so small that one feels that what he does personally makes a difference, is an effort well made. It is all too easy to be merely passive in a vast congregation.

As in drama, the fewer the props the greater the personal demands. Yet, one wonders whether most Christians are equal to the demands frequently imposed by small-group liturgies. Should they be the rule, or the exception? Further, does there not lurk the danger of elitism or cliquishness, when one's worship is carried out exclusively in the surroundings of friends or like-minded persons?

Doesn't the Christian belong to the wider community as well as to the smaller homogeneous one?

No univocal answer seems likely to be forthcoming. As we need a rhythm of more or less intense celebrations, I believe we need a rhythm of place. The smaller, informal place fills certain needs and expresses certain realities about Christian community. But so does the larger, somewhat more formal, more encompassing place. For as social beings, and still more as Christians, we belong to many communities, narrow and wide. Always to express simply one or other of these is a diminishment and possibly an evasion of responsibility.

The implications here are obvious, if complex. Some time ago, in an article, "New Style Parish" (*New Catholic World,* March/April 1972), I studied the Community of John the Evangelist, New Orleans. Inspired to some extent by that of John XXIII in Oklahoma City, this parish has no territorial boundaries, and accordingly no church or rectory. Almost by definition it is small, with only a hundred or so adult members. My initial enthusiasm led me to suggest that this was the ideal parish of the future. "No, I'm afraid not," replied the pastor; "it's much too tough for that."

It took time for me to grasp his point. Such a parish, with no geographical supports, drawing on the whole city, makes demands that only the full-time Christian can respond to. The very fact of no neighborhood means the effort of gathering at some distance from home. While this may seem normal in an automotive age, the fact remains that we tend to do most things (such as shopping, socializing, working when possible, going to school—witness part of the furor over bussing) near where we live. Even the neighborhood cinema remains something of the norm.

I hope that these reflections will not seem a veiled plea for a return to neo-gothic or neo-baroque ecclesiastical buildings. If at present relatively few elaborate churches are going up, we may reckon this a blessing. Most parishes are suffering a loss of fiscal nerve that makes architectural ambitions rather out of the question. Few pastors feel the assurance needed to launch into a full-scale building program. Today, thus, we hear few echoes of the old "edifice complex" complaint.

At the same time, new churches continue to be built and older ones to be updated. To verify this, all one need do is glance through issues of *Liturgical Arts Quarterly* over the past five years or so. True, an occasional mammoth building may be found, like the new San Francisco cathedral. But on the whole the newer churches are more modest, more functional, even more multipurpose. More and more pastors seem to recognize that the formula for the church building is not so much "the house of God" as the "house of the people of God." This is no mere verbal quibble, but a return to a more primitive and I believe more Christian understanding. For the earliest churches were not Constantinian basilicas, but more like homes where the people of God could gather in community for worship.[2]

Nor does this preclude a sense of celebration. While a parish may not need an elaborate "sacral" building, it does not follow that the only remaining option is one of barn-like sterility. (Yet, even a barn can be turned into a place of worship, provided the talents of a creative architect are elicited; witness the extraordinary success of the barn-turned-oratory at Grailville, Ohio.) Most of us, even austere Cistercians, need some visual and aural aids for our liturgical prayer.

But, given today's stress on constant change and even contrived obsolescence, much of this support can be, and perhaps should be, temporary. Hence the value of banners and hangings that can be changed seasonally or even weekly. Further, the abandonment of the fixed pew in favor of movable chairs or cushions opens the way to flexibility and variety more in keeping with the contemporary psyche.

So, I take it, if place still matters, it does not mean that total fixity is in order. One human value need not expell all others. If we need ceremony, we need something of a ceremonial site. And while this cannot be today at the sublime level of a Chartres or a Monreale, neither should it always be minimal or puritanical. Basically our worship must be in spirit and truth, but our spirit is incarnate and our truth far from disembodied.

Chapter Five

WHO

THERE was a time, not many years ago, when liturgy seemed totally centered on the altar and controlled by the priest. Or if not totally controlled by the priest, by some sort of conspiracy between priest and organist. Everything really important was done by the priest, while upstairs, in the back of the church, the organist performed a sort of concomitant or rival activity. But hardly anything happened in between.

Then appeared certain magic formulas—centered on the word "participation"—which were to solve all problems; congregations were to be transformed from "detached and silent spectators" (the phrase was from Pius X's 1903 *Motu Proprio* on sacred music) into instant participants. Somehow, everybody was suddenly called to do everything. From virtually nothing to virtually everything.

The consequences were not infrequently disastrous. Choirs were hastily disbanded, organists instructed to make everybody sing or say everything, or perhaps fired, to be replaced by ardent amateur guitar strummers. Silence, of course, became almost literally unmentionable. What was not done together (remember that amiable word "togetherness"?) was reckoned as selfishness, solipsism, the defunct Jesus-and-I school of spirituality, something not only un-Catholic but un-Christian. To be sure, thanks to inertia or latent good sense, this instant liturgy did not catch on everywhere. Even today, some parishes are still redolent of the "good old days."

It would be merely too facile to pin all these excesses on any single distortion of liturgy, unless possibly on the easy tendency to identify liturgy with any single one of its ingredients—what may be termed "nothing-but-ism." Many pastors, even bishops, having looked askance on the whole liturgical movement, judging it freakish or mildly lunatic, were caught off balance by the *Constitution on the Sacred Liturgy*. Still, with reluctant but blind submission to its letter or some of its letters, they proceeded forthwith to go about resolutely implementing it. The document was read selectively, with little attention paid to its background and complexity (not to say its internal compromises or contradictions). It should not be altogether surprising that what took place did take place.

Participation, however, means collegiality, not creeping homogenization. True, everybody is called upon to play a part, but a role remains a role. A "college" or "team" presupposes some definition of responsibilities; not everyone is expected or qualified to play quarterback. True, in baptism we are all made sharers in the one priesthood of Christ. Yet, although it is the major sacrament, baptism is not the only one. It is not mere Counter-reformation theology, but within very ancient Christian tradition (found in both East and West) to hold that certain functions in liturgy are relegated to priests—whether or not the term "priest" is ideal. St. Paul has something to say about this.[1]

Perhaps the shock was inevitable; in any case, one

hopes it will be in the long run salutary. There can be little doubt that too much had been made of vestments, incensing of priests, postures of clerical deference. Certain sets of symbols suggested that liturgy was of, for and by the clergy, with the laity reserved to a static, passive or almost irrelevant stance. Until recently, the laity were expected to be present but silent, even their responses relegated to chosen acolytes. Only the collection was theirs.

This realization, common enough today at least in theory, gradually gained currency during Vatican II and has become relatively commonplace today. However, when Emile Joseph de Smedt, bishop of Bruges, addressed the Council on the topic "Priesthood of All Believers," this important truth was at last put into focus after centuries of blurring.

It is not hard to imagine the raised episcopal eyebrows during his talk, and perhaps still higher eyebrows when Ernest Primeau, Bishop of Manchester, New Hampshire, spoke on the "Responsible Freedom of the Layman." Bluntly, Bishop Primeau alerted his fellows that today's layman, "aware of his own abilities, will no longer put up with being treated as a passive member submitting blindly to the authority of the church, as a 'silent sheep.' " For we "do not put enough emphasis on individual responsibility, on freedom of initiative, which must be recognized in laymen in a positive spirit; after all, they are members of the Mystical Body of Christ. They should not constantly be lectured about their duty of subjection and reverence as if their whole vocation were summed up in four words: believe, pray, obey and pay."[2]

Even today, despite progress, I would urge many of my priest confreres to continue pondering these two great speeches. Yet, despite the ultraclericalism long rampant in our country, we need some care when it comes to righting the balance in liturgy. For, the ordained priesthood (or whatever term one prefers) implies presidency, and while a "president" is not a "monarch," nor should his appearance smack of the Byzantine, he does have an identifiable role. Certain prayers have, so far as we can go back in the history of Christian worship, always been reserved to him. Thus, it is absurd to force entire congregations to read the traditionally priestly prayer—what used to be called the "canon," more properly the "eucharistic prayer."

Concelebration was another phenomenon that came suddenly upon the liturgical scene right after Vatican II. Praised as a form of eucharist "by which the unity of the priesthood is appropriately manifested," it, too, was expected to be the panacea against solipsism, against the abuse of "private" Masses. The difficulty, as I see it, about concelebration as it was quickly introduced was that it was introduced all too quickly. The "homework" had not been adequately done. For though the early church had practiced a sort of concelebration, and in the East the practice had been continued or developed, we in the West had little to go on. Our practice of new priests reciting all the words with the bishop during the ordination ceremony had nothing to do with the older tradition.[3]

So it was that the "new" ceremony (discussed briefly in the liturgical *Constitution*) did little more than break up the single eucharistic prayer, arbitrarily assigning portions to be said by individual priests. Little wonder that priests quickly became weary of this antisymbolic formula. Many, in fact, now concelebrate by simply expressing their presence, standing around the "principal concelebrant" in a sort of presbytery, much like that of the early church, when bishops celebrated surrounded by their priests. Again, the problem was that of undifferentiated roles, as though five or fifty priests could equally preside, simply by parceling out the presidential prayer.

Something of the same problem arose with regard to communion. From communion strictly under one kind, there were many who wanted to insist that everyone in every Mass should drink from the same cup. In small group liturgies, of course, there seems no problem, and as long as people with colds or contagious diseases abstain from the cup, the symbol of such sharing seems altogether fitting. Our Lord did say "all of you drink from this." But when it comes to hundreds of communicants, difficulties arise. Here, I suggest, we can learn once again from the East, where intinction (dipping the host in the chalice) has long been the practice. It retains most of the richness of the eucharistic symbol, while eliminating hygienic hazards of indelicacy.

Then again, there are those eager communicants who might be dubbed the "snappers"—so zestful are they to take rather than receive the host. I see no objection and many advantages to the practice of Christians communicating themselves (if the neologism be permitted). Our Lord did say "take and eat," and the normal way of sharing food with adults involves an element of taking.

Yet, to receive is a characteristic Christian role. In the catacomb of Santa Priscilla, the ancient Orante prays with extended arms, indicating reception of God's gifts. So, too, in communion the Christian is above all a recipient, and this position is well expressed by receiving the host from the priest, whose role here is to present it in God's name.

A number of ways may be suggested for doing this: from hand to hand, or from basket or paten to hand. In these ways the Christian's double role of activity and of reception are clearly symbolized.

Another area where confusion of roles has wrought havoc is, as suggested above, that of music. Music has many functions, perhaps chief among them being that of communitarian expression. The most primitive cave drawings suggest as much, and so far as I know, almost all religions have used music partly to draw the worshipping community together. Even in Islam, the muezzin summons the faithful to prayer, chanting musical formulas.

Congregational singing may not be quite so universal in the history of religions, but it is surely an effective means of heightening and intensifying the community experience. We have a great deal here as elsewhere to learn from the Lutheran tradition, with its stresses on Christian elements long unstressed among Catholics.

Yet, even in the Lutheran approach to music, congregational singing is never exclusive. Bach's hundreds of cantatas, as well as his Passions and other liturgical music, assign strong roles to choirs, soloists and instrumental participation. Once again it seems that a reaction in favor of congregational music was a seriously needed reaction. But like many reactions, it turned into an overreaction, as though all music had to be performed by everybody.

This excess arose out of a failure to examine the deepest traditions of liturgical music as well as the very phenomenology of music. The social function of music can take several forms. A group can be galvanized not merely by its own singing, but by intense listening to soloists or professional groups. We note this among young and old, in both "classical" and "pop" cultures. Listening does not necessarily mean passivity. Indeed, it can be a very high form of activity. And, while not all musical experiences should be merely "spectator" experiences, there remains a place for these too. Again, history and anthropology have something to suggest here: In music the soloist or expert has been an important figure, from the paleolithic to the present.

I am not lamenting the demise of most choirs as I recall them. It is generally romantic to suppose that the option lay between Gregorian chant as performed at Solesmes, or the great polyphonic tradition as kept alive in a few centers, and third-rate "folk" Masses.

The unromantic reality is that most of the chant actually heard was dismally droned out, while the polyphony was, on the whole, the derivative trivia of Carlo Rossini, Nicolai Montani, Pietro Yon or less. Once again, it may well be that the housecleaning that came about, with whatever gaucherie, was an indispensable step toward a healthier music for worship. Just as the *Motu Proprio* of Pius X helped to restore our vision of sacred music—badly, since it was abused by many people with merely antiquarian interests—there is no reason that the newer freedom should not lead to real growth.

This, however, presupposes considerable intelligence and a sense of what liturgical music is all about. It implies, too, the willingness to employ competent musicians, not merely persons of enthusiasm and good will. As long as parishes pay music directors less than they pay janitors, little can be expected. If Bach had not had a decent salary (he kept insisting on this), we should not have the Cantatas; if Palestrina had not, we should not have the

Masses or motets. If Boston College and the Cathedral of Providence did not offer equitable remuneration, the vast talents of an Alexander Peloquin could not have been dedicated to sacred music even now. Liturgy and knowledge and love of it cannot dispense with money. One reason why Protestant churches generally have better sacred music than Catholic churches in the United States is surely the accepted concept of Minister of Music, which we should do well to emulate. Our recent past has been scandalous indeed.[4]

Other forms of ministry are no less urgent. Who has not suffered through the dim ministrations of lectors and congregational directors who brought to their tasks only benevolence. Yet there is probably no parish in our country where professional radio or television announcers would not be honored to serve in these capacities. Almost as urgently as musicians, these professional speakers are needed and will continue to be needed. In perhaps most instances they would be happy to help us priests to fulfill our functions as well, since Holy Orders cannot alone supply for inability to communicate. As long as the liturgy could be harmlessly mumbled in arcane Latin, this need may not have been quite so apparent. Today, however, a badly mumbled service is not only intolerable; it is counterproductive and damaging. Here, too, much of the problem lies in the adequate understanding and acceptance of roles in worship.

Chapter Six

HOW

THIS chapter will inevitably be somewhat more casual and rambling than the others. It has more to do with implementation than with theory, perhaps with the peripheral rather than the core. Thus, it may be less consensual, more controversial, in that experiences vary widely among those specially involved in the liturgy. Further, while liturgical theory, thanks to pioneer work by Josef Jungmann, Romano Guardini, Gerald Ellard and others, has achieved something of a broad unanimity, practice is more experimental and will very likely continue in a state of flux, possibly for the rest of time.

Change, flexibility, pluriformity are very much with us, even among those most inclined to abide by directives and rubrics. In fact, the very term "rubric" sounds vaguely anachronistic, since the mood of Vatican II and its sequel has been pastoral rather than legalistic. Whereas, a decade ago we could use only one "canon," today four are in common use, with a great number about to be made official, to say nothing of the scores of others widely known.

All of this causes dismay among the unimaginative and unventuresome, who find it far more comfortable to be directed at every step. In the older style, one could raise one's voice only so loud, spread one's arms only so wide, bow no more than a required different number of degrees whether at the name of Jesus, or of Mary, or of the saint being commemorated. All was neatly fixed and undeviating. The person of the priest was not to intrude; his role was rigidly delineated, hieratic, impersonal. Only during the sermon was he given any latitude. Today, he must prepare not only the homily, but choices of scripture and prayers, and the general tonality of celebration. He cannot doff his personality during liturgy.

Accordingly, a new term has come into the liturgical vocabulary: taste. Planning a celebration, the priest (preferably with a wide measure of consultation) must sense what fits and what does not fit. He must have serious regard for the age, culture, needs of the specific congregation to be served. What may be quite acceptable in a cathedral during, say, a solemn ordination ceremony, would obviously be out of place in a liturgy directed to the spiritual requirements of a teen-age group at summer camp. What would seem stately and appropriate in one situation would be, in another, merely grotesque.

Further, since one man's taste is another man's kitsch, the priest can hardly ever fail to consult. He can no longer take refuge in Roman decrees or episcopal pronunciamentos. People have tasted flexibility and have a right to expect it. They know that if St. Mary's parish won't do something, neighboring St. Joseph's will. Happily gone is the total-slot uniformity that used to be such a leveler. The priest must learn a great deal about his constituencies, the portion of the people of God that he is serving on the given occasion.

Let us mention a simple example: the sign of peace. A

decade ago no problem arose. The priest simply said, in Latin, "May the peace of the Lord be always with you." This caused no embarrassment, since he had his back to the people anyway and their response—usually given only by the server—conveniently ended the whole affair. Only if other priests were in the sanctuary, on rare, special occasions, did he give the "Pax" to them, solemnly, rubrically, vestigially, with nothing approaching human warmth.

Today all is different. He asks the people to give each other some sign of peace, aware that the Archie Bunkers in the congregation will resent the entire business, thinking, if not muttering: "This is no place to shake hands! Church used to be a place where one could enjoy privacy; now they want us to start talking to everybody, and right before Communion, too!"

It seems obvious that no uniform solution to the "peace" problem can be expected. The size and homogeneity of the group will have much to say about this ceremony as about others. Possibly the "peace" could be offered at another point in the Mass—at the beginning, by way of symbolizing community; at the penitential rite, by way of symbolizing forgiveness and the prayer for mutual forgiveness; after Communion, as an expression of our unity in Christ; at the very end of Mass, in connection with the final blessing. Even now, I know of no rubric that forbids such options. But however or whenever it is done, it should not be redolent of mere formalism. It must be meant.

An experience that I enjoy most Sundays of the year may be mentioned here. During the Mass at a home for the very infirm and aged, the "peace" has become a most significant part of the entire liturgy. Elderly and infirm people love it—they enjoy the experience of touching and being touched, lovingly, compassionately. At no point does the sense of community become more intense. I suspect, too, that when the ceremony is properly introduced, even in the most conservative parishes, it becomes a true sign of Christian brotherhood.

The allied matter of posture constantly comes up for discussion. Is it better to stand during the Mass or Communion, or to kneel? History can afford hints in favor of either posture, as does the analysis of symbolism. Kneeling, however, is traditionally related to repentance and submission. During a penitential rite it seems altogether appropriate. However, the eucharistic prayer and communion rite are more expressive of joy and thanksgiving, and these are better expressed by standing. Further, even in the Roman rite of a few years ago, the priest always stood during these parts of the liturgy. Why, then, should not the faithful? Moreover, history informs us that this is the ancient tradition of the church.

And one step further back, in the very early church we can be sure that the liturgy was celebrated in a sitting or reclining posture. For small groups especially, sitting even now seems far more appropriate. In any case, no single posture possesses intrinsic sacrality, just as none is *per se* profane.

How much of the Mass should be sung? Before recent liturgical developments all was predetermined: If a Mass were "high," all of a prescribed number of parts had to be sung; if it were "low," the prescriptions were somewhat freer. Today we are expected to use judgment and taste.[1]

By way of tentative suggestions, let me propose that no more be sung than can be fittingly and effectively sung.

To be functional at all, music must be at least minimally agreeable. Especially does this apply to the priest, who is given no special vocal charism by ordination. Anyone who has spent endless hours trying to teach chant to unmusical candidates for the priesthood will recall the anguish of teacher and pupil, meandering through the mazes of Preface or Pater Noster.

Fortunately, today nothing has to be sung by the priest, and in most cases, I believe, it would be better if nothing were sung by him. The energy can be much better spent in learning how to read intelligibly and effectively. Another more easily acquired art is that of using the public address system. In all but very small group situations, this art is a necessity, not a luxury.

This is not, of course, to belittle the role of soloists during the liturgy. They are indispensable in providing leadership, for intonations, for psalms or psalm-like canticles to which the congregation or choir provides responses. The point is, quite simply, that there is no connection between solo performance and priesthood. In Judaism, for example, much stress is placed on the cantor's role, this does not usurp the distinct function of preaching or collective prayer. Again, however, we can hardly expect a soloist of high competence to play a significant role gratis; too many years of professional work and consequent expense have gone into his or her preparation.

Still less should the choir be abolished or diminished in importance. The liturgical Constitution is quite explicit on this matter: "The treasure of sacred music is to be preserved and fostered with very great care. Choirs may be diligently promoted" (#114). Of all passages in the Constitution perhaps none has been so consistently neglected or "silenced" out of existence.

I have little doubt that this entire section of the Constitution was something of a pastiche of conflicting purposes. This is notably the case three paragraphs later, where it is stated that Gregorian chant, "other things being equal, should be given pride of place in liturgical services." What precisely is meant by "pride of place"?

After some reflection, I have come to believe that Fr. Lucien Deiss has given the most perceptive explanation. He concludes a discussion of the Council and chant: "With considerable prudence the editors of the Constitution judged that in order to obtain new objectives and open uncharted ways it would be diplomatic to make certain concessions on the subject of Latin and Gregorian."[2] For later in the same Constitution, in the chapter on sacred art, we read that "the Church has not adopted any particular style as her very own. . . . The art of our own days, coming from every race and region, shall also be given free scope. . . . It will thereby be enabled to contribute its own voice to that wonderful chorus of praise in honor of the Catholic faith sung by great men in times gone by." This latter quotation is clearly more in accord with the entire Constitution, as well as with the most significant document of the entire Council, that *On the Church in the Modern World.*

It is not hard to imagine howls of dismay or cries of "traitor" from friends with whom I was long associated in pre-Council sacred music, or those whom I taught Gregorian chant. My enthusiasm for this great music style is in no sense diminished with time; rather, the contrary. Nor do I believe that Gregorian, or other ancient styles, no longer has any relevance. The precise opposite may, in fact, be the case.[3]

For, at any time within memory, how many people were actually served by Gregorian chant? Surely the monks of Solesmes and some other abbeys were; and there were the privileged few who possessed the opportunity and musical sophistication to enjoy such music performed in the bastions of Gregorian culture. I am happy to have been one of them. But I believe that today we are in a more real, hence more liturgical, situation. Recordings are available and can be enjoyed as perhaps never before. Further, today's young people, accustomed to oriental and modal music, find Gregorian far more fascinating than did young people two decades ago.

From a strictly liturgical viewpoint, I find no objection to the selective use of Gregorian chant during worship. Provided it is sensitively performed, it can serve. And, as long as a lector or leader explains what is being sung, it can be a true vehicle of liturgical prayer. Even without explanation, it can be used effectively as "pure music," much like organ music, without explicit denotation.

This may be the place to insist again that music performs several functions, both in life and specifically in liturgy. It can be performed, and it can be listened to. At no time in the history of Catholic liturgical music, not even in medieval monasteries or cathedrals, was everything sung by everybody. Those magnificent Gradual melodies, to mention just a few Gregorian chants, were never meant to be sung by entire congregations. Even at Solesmes Abbey, they are sung today by specialists, and are contemplated by everyone else. Today, too, I find them enthusiastically appreciated by college students, again provided they are done competently.

The liturgical Constitution insisted on the "treasure of sacred music," which "is to be preserved and fostered with very great care." No one, surely, would interpret this to mean that the liturgy is primarily an instrument for preserving the art of the past. True, it has an important pedagogical function—the living catechesis of God's word. Further, cultural historians like Christopher Dawson make much of its civilizing function, especially in ages not widely literate.[4] Nor should one be so puritanical as to exclude or eschew the culturally elevating effects of sacred art, architecture or music. But to lament the abandonment of Gregorian or other early music simply because of some real or supposed cultural deprivation is to confuse means and ends.

The very pluralism of today's world, however, should make it possible for the music of many styles and periods to speak to us as never before. Bach's contemporaries heard almost no music except of that time; so did Beethoven's. But concert halls today are no strangers to music of many continents and even of many centuries, sometimes during the same programs. Recently, while chatting with Nino Rota (composer of music for the Fellini and other Italian films), I asked what music he listened to at home. "Bach, Mozart, George Gershwin, Dallapicola, the Beatles, Rolling Stones—in fact, all kinds of music," he replied. Given today's media, it is almost impossible not to be somewhat familiar with all kinds of music. Never before has so much Bach or Mozart been heard by so many young and older people, to say nothing of so many diverse kinds of "pop" music.

So it is that I find no contradiction or inconsistency in using many forms of music even in a single liturgy. A recent example in point occurred among a group of artist confreres, when we celebrated the liturgy in the Gesù,

Rome, at the altar of St. Ignatius on his feast day. Music ranged from Gregorian chant, to a Mass by Dufay, a motet by Josquin, a Sanctus by Alexander Peloquin, and a new folk composition by Bob Fabing. True, the styles were different, but no one seemed disturbed by this, since all were of excellent quality. Had we been equipped, doubtless we should have used electronic music as well, with no compelling reason to feel it incongruous either.

It should be obvious from what has been said that liturgical music today can, and perhaps should, be diversified. But it should be no less obvious that not everything can or should be sung, much less by everybody. The *Sanctus,* I believe, should ideally be sung by congregations, with or without supporting choirs and instruments; perhaps the more the better, as suggesting the whole of creation. *Amens,* too, should be sung—not every *Amen,* but at least the one ratifying the eucharistic prayer, the so-called *Great Amen.* And why not sing the doxology—"For the kingdom, etc."—and, when possible, at least some of the "Glory to God," say a refrain, while the choir or soloist carry on the entire text?

I should also like to see the *Kyrie* restored, not necessarily in an elaborate form, but as the response to the Prayers of the Faithful. For "Kyrie eleison," more than a prayer for forgiveness, is really wider in meaning: something like "Lord, hear our prayer," or "Hear us, O Lord." This is its original use in the East (from where it was brought to our rite), and its restoration would be appropriate as a link with other Christians and with our own tradition, much as we have kept "Amen" and "Alleluia."

If these easier and briefer acclamations can best be sung by entire congregations, music of great elaboration should be sung by skilled choirs or soloists. Further, the rich repository of motets and Masses from the past, both Latin and vernacular, can be drawn on.

However, there is clear need, too, for new music, and while not very much of the music recently written for liturgy is of high quality, there is some, and it is of considerable stylistic variety. Apart from Stravinsky, Poulenc, Vaughan Williams, Edmund Rubbra, and other older modern composers, the repertory is constantly being enlarged by Alexander Peloquin, Richard Yardumian, Daniel Pinkham, Richard Felciano, Lou Harrison, Clarence Rivers and others. The works of Lucien Deiss, Joseph Gelineau, Bernard Huijbers and other Europeans have been increasingly translated and made available. We may not be living in a "golden age" (if indeed such an age ever existed), but neither are we living in a musical wasteland.

Other arts, too, should play their part in modern liturgies. Poetry is enjoying a popularity today far greater than at most times since Gutenberg, and oral readings may be more widely attended now than at any time since Chaucer. Readings at the time of the homily, or at other appropriate points, may be very effective. One such example is proposed in the final chapter.

The dance in liturgy may strike certain of my contemporaries as inherently blasphemous. Yet, the ritual solemnity of an old-style pontifical Mass was surely a stylized dance, and everyone has heard of the liturgical dance at Seville. To be sure, it will take on different forms, according to the age or temperament of the congregation. But I have seen both dance and mime most effectively used, as for example in the cathedral of Oakland, California, during summer liturgies for the young. One such dance included an abundance of balloons, both during processions and swinging solemnly to and fro like incense during the Mass itself. Gesture, after all, and dance differ not so much in kind as in degree, and even a rigorist will not exclude all gesture.

The problem, again, is one of appropriateness and taste. But appropriateness and taste must not be identified with blandness. If the expression is merely bland, the symbolism projected will be that of a dull, effete or even defunct religion. Here perhaps least of all can fixed rules be set down. Consultation and careful planning, and later feedback must indicate the way.

I see no difficulty, though considerable effort, in the liturgical use of projections, whether stills or films. A number of modern churches are equipped for these, but even older buildings may be adapted. Appropriate visual aids may be used during the scripture readings, during acclamations, before or after Mass itself. An entire congregation of Christians have grown up in the TV age and are seldom without the visual supports that used to be rare—or rather, used to be permanently fixed in stained glass, frescoes or statuary.

A simple and not too shocking way to introduce this, and one I have long found effective, is the projecting of Christmas slides during carols before Midnight Mass. Even the least radical of people have found this easy to adjust to, and, once the technique was accepted in principle, could accept even more.

It is obvious that during informal, nonofficial "liturgies" taste will suggest far more imaginative procedures. I have in mind prayer groups, pentecostal meetings and other forms of social prayer not officially liturgical. Since such smaller gatherings are largely the creation of like-minded people, with similar spiritual needs and preparation, there is less likelihood of mere shock or discomfort. The growing literature on the charismatic movement has covered this matter so fully that I see no need to go beyond recommending Donald Gelpi's balanced works on the subject.[5]

The conversion experience which many Catholics have experienced in the charismatic renewal is one that is subject to several possible theological interpretations. Recognizing some ambivalence here, Father Gelpi draws on the wealth of material available in the theological and sacramental traditions to cast light upon the Pentecostal experience. His books also use the Pentecostal experience to throw light on sacramental piety and practice. One can and should enrich the other.

The charismatic renewal has provided the impetus for a number of liturgical adaptations, all well within the guidelines of renewal set down by Vatican II. Liturgies celebrated for charismatic Catholics not infrequently include a long period of prayer after communion, punctuated by hymns, prayers, words of prophecy and teaching. General prayers for healing can also be incorporated into the prayers of the faithful.

It may, in fact, be said that the tendency within the movement is to keep carefully within the present directives of the church. Charismatic Catholics as a whole are somewhat less given to experimentation in liturgy and more to a concern that liturgy, whatever its external form might take, should be genuinely "Spirit-filled."

While most of our attention here has gone into the eucharistic life of the church—since it is our everyday sacrament—a word or so should be suggested about the other sacraments, despite their relative infrequency. Theologians relate them so closely to the eucharist that they may be thought of as, in a sense, satellite sacraments.

Par excellence, however, baptism is *the* sacrament of initiation. Unfortunately, though sound theological reasons can be offered in defense, baptism is normally received by the person at a time when his awareness is nil. As long as the present practice of the church favors infant baptism, the initiation ceremony will make a more immediate impression on family and friends than on the neophyte Christian.[6]

Even so, the liturgy of baptism should not be given Cinderella status. Nor need it be. Few moments of family life can be so significant as that of baptism. In some families, in fact, it may provide a rare contact with the rest of the church. Hence the importance of careful preparation and adaptation, and as far as possible the avoidance of mass-production lines.

Its relationship to the eucharist can well be expressed by having baptism during Mass, especially at the Easter Vigil or at Sunday Mass—a reminder that every Sunday stands for Easter. But even where this may not prove possible, some relation to the altar can and ideally should be visibly expressed. One of the most moving baptismal ceremonies I can recall took place in the cathedral of Monreale, near Palermo. I had dropped in to see the cathedral and was very much captivated by the liturgical style and flexibility of the priest conducting the ceremony (I later discovered that he was a distinguished historian). Since the larger family was present, the celebrant made sure that everyone could hear and understand everything. Addressing his comments to the baby, he guided the family procession from the baptistry to the high altar. "And now, Luigi," he explained, "here is the altar where you will make your first Communion, where you will be confirmed and where you will be married." Far from perfunctory, the ceremony became an exciting family event.

Confirmation has lately been coming more to the fore as the sacrament completing initiation. It is a special moment for making the young Christian more aware of his Christian vocation, responsibility, privileges. Today we find some difference in practice, certain dioceses insisting that it be given early in the child's conscious life; others assert that it come later in adolescence or together with graduation. The latter procedure seems to make more sense, since children can be constantly reinitiated in the Christian life by the eucharist, whereas at the beginning of adulthood a special sacrament of initiation and personal commitment seems more necessary.

Matrimony can be made more meaningful in a number of ways. Time spent with the celebrants (the bride and groom) can help prepare a ceremony that will make a deep impression on both them and their friends. The choice of readings and music, the assignment of liturgical roles (for example, having bride and groom do the readings, and addressing them both to each other and to the assembly), the matter of positions in the sanctuary, can all make a considerable difference. One approach that I have found useful is that of having bride and groom stand at the altar facing the people—a clear symbol that they, and not the priest, are the ministers of the sacrament. This can be made even more intelligible if bride and groom approach their place as celebrants from different sides of the altar, and then return to their places after the vows arm in arm.

The sacrament of penance offers problems and special opportunities today. Many of the young especially have no interest in hiding in an anonymous confessional, but prefer a situation more like that of counseling. Newer churches, in fact, often provide for this option. But the social aspect of the sacrament needs visible expression. Penance services, with group prayers as well as generic declarations of sinfulness, can do a great deal toward relating the sacrament to the whole people of God. The sacrament can thus become a true community celebration adjusted to the full needs of penitents, both social and private.

Even the sacrament of the sick, now happily no longer called "extreme unction," can be more clearly related to the community. It can, in fact, be made a family event, or even a full congregational one, and received in church, with the full prayerful and moral support of the parish as well as friends. The mood is, thus, not one of fear but of Christian consolation.

Happily, one of the most immediate consequences of Vatican II in liturgy was a total revision of the rites surrounding burial. Suggested prayers and ceremonies are now related to the wake, with stress on immortality and sharing in Christ's resurrection, rather than the threat and gloom of death. Not that these new rites need exclude the rosary, which many people find comforting and participatory; indeed, the quiet, rhythmical, almost incantatory character of a rosary recited in a group creates a sort of verbal music conducive to prayerfulness and peace. In this regard it is especially important, I believe, to respect the sensibilities of older people—most of all the bereaved. Yet, provided the new, resurrection-centered liturgical prayers are sensitively said, and the rich scriptural texts effectively proclaimed, the elderly too find the entire funeral service an enormous aid in time of distress.

Once again, the "how" of the liturgy seems to center on the people who are to participate and be served by it. Worship is, of course, focused on God and any worship that is not God-centered can be no more than bogus. But we know that God did not give us sacraments—or, indeed, the church as sacrament—except for our good. If we insist on taste and appropriateness in liturgical matters, it is, however, not as though God needed these; we do.

But since we are a pluralistic, diversified, changing people, we cannot be effectively helped in any single univocal way. Granted, what we have in common is deeper than what distinguishes us from one another. But gaps remain, both of generation and of culture, and these need respecting if our life of worship is to be really alive and not mummified.

Yet our pluralism cannot remain comfortably enclosed in our neighborhood, be that neighborhood strictly parochial or even extended to encompass our nation or the entire Western World. The parable of the Good Samaritan today has a planetary meaning, very much including what we condescendingly call the Third World. It must be more than coincidence that most of the privileged moments of divine revelation, and most of all the Incarnation itself, took place on or near the bridge that unites the three continents that are our ancestral homes. If most of the Third World is in two of these three continents, much of the fault may lie not only in various sorts of imperialism, but also in the apathy and unconcern of so many Christians.

It is not merely that we have been ungenerous toward

our unseen brothers and sisters, quick to take and slow to share. But we have also been slow, or perhaps too arrogant, to learn from them. True, Christ is one, but inevitably our vision of him has been filtered through a culture which, for all its strengths, is not universal. Modern missiologists, from Pierre Charles to the present, have been urging us to widen and enrich this vision. Most recently, John Moffitt, American and former Hindu monk, has carried us one important step further in *The Journey to Gorakhpur,* where the subtitle bears a timely challenge: "An Encounter With Christ Beyond Christianity." Our liturgy of the future will surely be richer and more broadly human because of these insights.

Meantime, apart from reading and praying, we can palpably help those engaged in the Christ life in the Third World. A few years ago I did a small piece on the work of Brother Andrew in the worst slums of Calcutta, where he and a group of young Indians have dedicated themselves to the most destitute of their brothers.[7] An enterprising pastor in Sioux Falls (S.D.) read the account from the pulpit. In consequence, the parishioners asked to give their entire Christmas Mass offering to Brother Andrew and his work. Seldom, I suspect, has a Mass offering done so much good or been such a tangible liturgical overflow into Christian witness.

APPENDIX

WHILE a fair variety of Eucharistic Prayers (what used to be referred to as "canons" or "anaphoras") can be found, few literary liturgists have tried their hands at a possible restructuring of the liturgy as a whole.

I am happy to present, as a sample of the sort of development that may be foreseen, an original composition by a confrere, Francis P. Sullivan, S.J. Fr. Sullivan is a well-known and widely-published poet. He has achieved considerable success, too, in adapting liturgies for special groups—students, artists and the like. The one here offered strikes me as one of his most successful, fresh in design and imagery, yet deeply traditional.

EUCHARISTIC LITURGY

Cel: Let us pray.

Con: Father,
hallowed be thy name.
Thy kingdom come.

Give us each day our daily bread;
and forgive us our sins,
for we ourselves forgive everyone
who is indebted to us;
and lead us not into temptation.

Lector: Open our hands.

We have closed them.
We have closed them on golden sand.
We have made our loves into crumpled
   bills held in pockets against the crowd.
We have gone by beggars afraid,
closing our fists tight as sealed kegs.

Open our hands.

We have tried possessing the rain.
We possess our homes with walls, with
   laws, with signs forbidding trespass.
We grip status as men gripped swords once
to create fear and gain wealth.

Open our hands.

We have licked them for water in the
   desert and found dust in our mouths.
We have touched our children,
turned them to gold and our hearts broke.
We have washed our hands clean
of dirt and avarice,
and so let others tumble over falls

to some destiny of their own.

Open us.

Our eyes we have boarded up;
no one looks in; no one looks out.

We cannot hear men breaking
as bottles thrown from speeding cars.

We hug ourselves and wait for you

to show us the ways of sand,
to show us the ways of love,
ways to touch, to see
your mercies without number,
your face
where we kiss, or comb,
or straighten in death,
or in birth;

to know that fear
is the edge of a storm passing,

that our hands
can spread blessings like rain,
can turn the spirit of others gold
with a touch only love can work.

Open us.

Stretch out your hand, and

we will be created
and renew the face of the earth.

Lector: I John 4:7–21

Lector: Rivers carry sludge to the sea.
The air washes smoke from burning ovens.
Fire has danced great heaps of refuse
down.
The earth has taken our dead.
Yet our pyramids grow upward, outward,
thoughts, scaffolding, penthouse, church;
men below set the stones.
at the wave of our hands or our breath.

Grain is at our feet,
the vines we only hear of,
the air that cools the ground
or takes exhausts away for scattering
somewhere.
We are served.
We are served life in every breath,
in every love, in the colors that settle
or fly like feeding birds,
in the joy that has its own well inside us
we cannot find.

We are served and know not
who gives the ground we fence,
the oil, the gas, the steel, the power
we charge for,

the cliffs and beaches below cliffs,
sounds we shape to music,
bodies we sway to dance,
blood that races with passion,
men and women who lash themselves to
  wisdom
in the storms we make and speak the one
  truth;

And we know not why,
except we love
how we are gathered from the ground
as every gift is,
how we are shaped and torn and healed,
are dipped in promises of life
the way hands or feet or head are dipped
  in water
here in this earth;

except we wait
for the word that makes it plain
who serves us life and why,

for the word that makes love
a reason in itself,
the beginning and the end.

Lector: John 13:1–17

Offertory

Con: We open our hands to you, Father;
we open our lives.

1st Read: Our bread is a mortal life, days we consume
until no more remain.

2nd Read: Our wine is a mortal life, children and
children's children until no more remain.

1st/2nd Read: Father, we share with you our bread, our
wine because Jesus did who is your only
son. We share with you the vineyards,
the grainfields, the cities, the faces of
men, because Jesus did.
We share our sin with you. We share our
love that is a candle in winds. We share
our death with you because Jesus did
who is your only son.

1st Read: He made bread speak his body.

2nd Read: He made wine speak his blood,

1st/2nd Read: and the love that moved you,
and the love that moved him,
whom he gave,
whom he called his Spirit and yours.

Cel: Holy spirit, make this bread and wine we

give the body and blood of Jesus.

Con: You moved over the earth and made it.
You watched us unmake it.
You filled the Virgin with a son.
You named him God-with-us.
You opened our eyes to see him.
You stood with him in death.
You brought him back from among the dead.

Cel: Holy Spirit, make this bread and wine we give the body and blood of Jesus.

Canon

Cel: On the night before he died,
at his last supper,
Jesus took bread,
until then the bread of the passing of the Lord,
the bread given hungry crowds on the mountain,
the bread of his own prayer to the father;

he blessed it, he broke it, and said:

Take this and eat it; it is my body;
it will be broken for you.

Later in that supper before he died,

Jesus took wine,
until then the wine of the wedding feast,
the wine of the parable of the owner of the vineyard
and his son who was killed,
the wine of the kingdom to come;

he blessed it, and handed the cup of it
to them saying,

Take this and drink it; it is my blood;
it will be poured out for you
to forgive sins, yours and the multitudes;
it is my promise;

and when you bless bread and wine
from now on,
remember you renew this promise I make
to forgive all sin.

Con: We open our hands, Father; we open our lives;
we accept this bread and wine,
the body and blood of Jesus, who died for our sins,
who rose for our justification,
who lives with you now forever.
You have made him present here to us
through your Holy Spirit.

Communion

Under both species. To be given out by celebrant(s), by men and by women.

Hymn to the Father of Jesus

The fields, the lilies that grow wild,
the sparrows have a care in you;
grains of wheat speak of your providing;
wells in our desert places tell your life.
The hairs of our heads are counted,
the thoughts of our hearts are seen and
open to you as valleys are to the wind.

Hilltop cities speak of your presence;
their narrow gates, their streets are your
grief
and your hope who shape mansions for us.
The crooked limbs have a care in you,
the stopped eyes and ears and tongues;
the smashed ware of love invites you,
your hands to piece us together,
the hands of Jesus whom you sent.
From the rising of the sun to its setting,
through the nights that follow, your care
touches our fevers with a cool cloth,
our joys with arms put around us,
our fears with fingers that still babbling
lips.
Our liberty has a care in you.

You have watched many roads looking
for us to come home. You have sat
with the sinner and dropped your hands
helpless between your knees and waited;
you have trailed your fingers in the dust
as Jesus did one time condemning no one.
You have set the bread of life near us.
You have taken the sands of the seashore
and said count my days, days I share
with you, days of my Son and Spirit.
We praise you for your care, we bless you.

The Gift of Peace

Cel: In this communion, accept the peace of
Jesus,
whoever of you is in doubt,
whoever is helplessly in sin,
whoever has joy and searches its roots,
whoever wants to wake up to creation.

We have many witnesses:
Mary his mother,
disciples who went down to Emmaus,
Magdalene who saw him,
Peter and John and the Apostles,
Thomas among them.

They heard him say, "Peace be with you,"
and doubts went away,

and sins blew away like chaff,
and joy burst through time,
and death had no more sting.

He gave them that gave to give on.

In his name, in the name of all who
witnessed his gift from the beginning
to now, I offer you the peace of Jesus.
May it fill your hearts.

Con: May his peace fill your heart as well.

Petitions

Cel: Let us ask this peace for all men from Our Lord.

Con: We ask this from you Jesus.

Cel: That the violent of heart may give up killing, may find the meekness you have blessed.

Con: We ask this from you Jesus.

Cel: That the misers of the earth, of its goods, its pleasures, its places, its power, may find the poor whom you have blessed and raise them.

Con: We ask this from you Jesus.

Cel: That those who love wisdom, wherever, may have the pure heart you have blessed and your courage to set men free.

Con: We ask this from you Jesus.

Cel: That those who have your truth may learn to wash this world's feet as a sign of your great love and your gift of grace.

Con: We ask this from you Jesus.

Other petitions . . .

Reflections from the congregation, or a brief homily from the celebrant.

Conclusion

Cel: Be the green in the trees all men see,
and their copper and red and gold.

Be the cities clearing in the sun,
of their racket that frays our spirit,
of their greed that leaves us broken.

Be a change of seasons for men.
Be the cross of their city.

We will not fear a final autumn.
Our lives will not scatter like horns
against lights and aimless crowds.

We will tell street corners of you,
and windows who talk in the late sun.

We will tell every season your name.
We will instruct wheat and vines.

The earth is no spent top,
nor its people brief lightning at night.

We have bread that says it is so,
and wine, and water, and breath.
We have oil and hands to bless our senses.
We have love that lives in words,
and words that lie down with the dead.

We have creation given back to our grasp,
and every man to our heart.

Send us Lord with this your gift
to every place, to every one,

to announce your glory
that was, and is, and ever shall be,
world without end. Amen.

NOTES

Introduction

1. No one should be surprised if I strongly recommend as preparatory reading some recent book on the church, without which liturgy can hardly be discussed. For this purpose the reader can do no better than read or reread *What a Modern Catholic Believes About the Church* by Andrew Greeley.

2. Anyone curious about such antiquarian matters may find articles of mine on the subject back in *Orate Fratres* (May, 1947) and in *Worship* (March, 1961). Now "safe" and even bland, these articles once caused controversy.

Chapter One

1. For the full text of the Constitution, see the handy paperback edition of *The Documents of Vatican II* (Ed. Walter M. Abbott. The America Press. 1966). My introduction and commentary is quite uncomplicated, and, I hope, easy to read. Another quite untechnical treatment of the Constitution, together with the full text, may be found in my volume *Our Changing Liturgy* (Hawthorn. 1966).

2. A rich contemporary bibliography may be found in *Liturgy: Self-Expression of the Church* (Ed. Herman Schmidt. Herder and Herder. 1972).

3. The theme of liturgy overflowing into life has been a constant one among liturgists, perhaps starting with Gerald Ellard's classic *Liturgy and Life.* Entire sessions of the North American Liturgical Conference were dedicated to the social implications of liturgy. A simple treatment of this theme may be found in my recent volume, *Worship and Witness* (Bruce-Collier-Macmillan. 1970), designed as a discussion manual for adult groups.

4. For the liturgy, notably the Mass, as sacrifice, I recommend the treatment in *A New Catechism: Catholic Faith for Adults* (Herder and Herder. 1967), especially pages 332–347. Somewhat more difficult is Karl Rahner's volume *The Celebration of the Eucharist* (Herder and Herder. 1967).

Chapter Two

1. The Constitution is quite explicit about this (#12): "The spiritual life, however, is not confined to participation in the liturgy. The Christian is assuredly called to pray with his brethren, but he must also enter into his chamber to pray to the Father in secret (cf. Mt. 6:6)."

2. The phenomenal success of Bach's *Jonathan Livingston Seagull* in the past year or so, to say nothing of *The Velveteen Rabbit* and *The Little Prince* some years ago, suggests the perduring need of symbol and myth even at a semisecular level.

3. *A New Catechism* develops the themes of this chapter simply and perceptively, especially pp. 252–256.

Chapter Three

1. Chapter 5 of the Constitution treats of the Liturgical Year. In #107 it requires that the calendar "be revised so that the traditional customs and discipline of the sacred seasons can be preserved or restored to meet the conditions of modern

times." In the following paragraph stress is placed on "the feasts of the Lord in which the mysteries of salvation are celebrated . . . and given the preference which is due over the feasts of the saints."

2. *The Paschal Mystery* (Alba House. 1969) is a rich but readable series of texts from ancient liturgies and other early passages from the Church Fathers, edited by A. Hamman. It helps to put Sunday and Easter into true perspective.

3. Many of these are available in Robert F. Hoey's volume *The Experimental Liturgy Book* (Herder and Herder. 1969) and, together with original prayers for Sundays and larger occasions, in *Eucharistic Liturgies* (Ed. by John Gallen. Newman Press. 1969), an outgrowth of the interesting work that was being done at Woodstock College, New York City, before its untimely demise.

4. This book is also published by Newman as part of the series "Studies in American Pastoral Liturgy." Another book which I enthusiastically recommend is Helen McLoughlin's *My Nameday: Come for Dessert* (Liturgical Press, 1962). The late Mrs. McLoughlin, a housewife, presents hundreds of recipes (both for soul and body) to help youngsters celebrate the cycle of saints. Liturgical in the broadest sense.

5. The Tasaday people of Mindinao seem to have no ceremony. This, as far as we can judge at present, may be related to their lack of the sense of time or seasons. In such a life, every day and place seems equally sacred, save for great events like marriage. See articles in *National Geographic* August, 1972, and *New York Times Magazine,* Oct. 8, 1972.

Chapter Four

1. *A Guide to Christian Europe* (Hawthorn. 1963; reprinted 1972 by Loyola University Press, Chicago).

2. See article "The Place of Liturgical Worship," by Godfrey Diekmann, in *The Church and the Liturgy: Liturgy Vol.* 2 (Concilium: Paulist. 1965) and R. Kevin Seasoltz, *The House of God* (Herder and Herder. 1963).

Chapter Five

1. A scholarly, brief discussion of priesthood may be found in *Sacramentum Verbi: An Encyclopedia of Biblical Theology* (Ed. by J. B. Bauer. Herder and Herder. 1970), vol. 2, pp. 700–709. For a fuller treatment see James A. Mohler, *The Origin and Evolution of the Priesthood* (Alba. 1969).

2. The splendid texts may be found in *Council Speeches of Vatican* II (ed. by Hans Küng, Yves Congar and Daniel O'Hanlon. Paulist. 1964).

3. The Constitution treats of concelebration in paragraphs 57 and 58. The only rather full English treatment known to me is Jean C. McCowan's *Concelebration* (Herder and Herder. 1963).

4. I have treated this favorite theme of mine in a number of articles, viz. "The Priest As Patron" in *Liturgical Arts Quarterly* (XXIX, pp. 65–66). A fuller and more recent discussion can be found in Henry Raynor's volume *A Social History of Music* (Schocken. 1972), notably in the chapters titled "The Reformation and the Counter-Reformation" and "Churches, Cantors and Choirs."

Chapter Six

1. The most useful treatment of music in liturgy at the present moment is *Crisis in Church Music?* (The Liturgical Conference. 1967), especially the opening essay, "Music and Liturgy in Evolution," by Abbot Primate Rembert Weakland, where many balloons are deftly punctured.

2. In *Concile et Chant Nouveau* (Levain. 1968), pp. 273–283. Other important postconciliar books on church music, not yet translated, are Gino Stefani, *L'Acclamation de Tout un Peuple* (Fleurus. 1967), and *Le Chant Liturgique apres Vatican II* (Fleurus. 1966), with contributions by Joseph Gelineau, Helmut Hucke, René Reboud and other European leaders in the field.

3. I have argued this point in a number of articles, including one in the *New Catholic Encyclopedia*, "Music, Sacred," (Vol. 10, pp. 97–99) and more recently in "Liturgical Music for Today," in *America*, 11/14/70.

4. For example, see Dawson's classics, *The Making of Europe* (Meridian. 1945), *Religion and the Rise of Western Culture* (Image. 1950), *The Formation of Christendom* (Sheed and Ward, 1962), the latter being the first set of his Harvard lectures.

5. Donald Gelpi, *Pentecostalism: A Theological Viewpoint* (Paulist. 1971) and *Pentecostal Piety* (Paulist. 1972).

6. See Arthur McCormack, *Christian Initiation* (Hawthorn. 1969).

7. When asked how to reach Brother Andrew, I suggest that correspondence be sent c/o Mrs. L. Tevis, 1475 E. Mendocino St., Altadena, Calif. 19001.